Body Braille

Body Braille

Poems

Beth Gylys

Iris Press
Oak Ridge, Tennessee

Copyright © 2020 by Beth Gylys

All rights reserved. No portion of this book may be reproduced in any form or by any means, including electronic storage and retrieval systems, without explicit, prior written permission of the publisher, except for brief passages excerpted for review and critical purposes.

COVER ARTWORK:
León Ferrari, "Untitled" (2004), 22 X 14.5 cm
Poem: "Unión libre" by André Breton,
trans. Aldo Pellegrini, written in Braille over a photo by Ferdinando Scianna.
Collection: Alicia y León Ferrari
Copyright: FALFAA – CELS Agreement

The Center for Legal and Social Studies (CELS) is an Argentinian human rights organization founded in 1979 which operates nationally and internationally to promote human rights and social justice. To support CELS' work for the protection and promotion of justice and social inclusion go to: https://www.cels.org.ar/web/en/dona/

BOOK DESIGN: Robert B. Cumming, Jr.

Iris Press
www.irisbooks.com

Library of Congress Cataloging-in-Publication Data

Names: Gylys, Beth A., author.
Title: Body braille : poems / Beth Gylys.
Description: Oak Ridge, Tennessee : Iris Press, [2020] | Summary: "Body Braille by Beth Gylys is a collection that explores the failures and complications of existing in the world as a sentient being. Broken into five sections, four of the first five focus around a particular sense: touch, taste, vision/sight, and hearing. The book's final section—comprised of a crown of elegiac sonnets—follows a man after he loses his wife as he fights through the initial stages of grief. The collection—bookended by poems of intimacy and death—moves through the senses, reimagining the possibilities and failures of bodily experience and ending in death/life after excruciating loss. The collection is one undergirded by loss but also threaded through with resilience, a resilience that expresses itself as humor, as defiance, as longing, and as survival. Ultimately, the collection attempts to gain purchase on our humanity through its exploration of sensual and bodily experience"— Provided by publisher.
Identifiers: LCCN 2020013936 | ISBN 9781604542608 (paperback)
Subjects: LCGFT: Poetry.
Classification: LCC PS3607.Y58 B63 2020 | DDC 811/.6—dc23
LC record available at https://lccn.loc.gov/2020013936

Acknowledgments

Many thanks to the editors and staff of the following publications in which these poems first appeared:

32 Poems: "Soldier Heart"
Atlanta Review: "Wine: The Liquid Cure for Tax Time"
Barrow Street Review: "Working Your Way to The Top"
Birmingham Review: "Made Bed"
Chattahoochee Review: "A Friendship" and "Conundrum"
Cimarron Review: "House Purchase"
Connotations: "Anglerfish," "Our Father of Perpetual Sadness," and "When I Am Blind,"
Cortland Review: "Monastic"
Crab Orchard Review: "Market Forces" (Under the title "The Mount Washington Kroger is Out of Bananas")
Lake Effects: "Scaffold"
Muse/A: "Not Exactly" and "Ways of Falling"
New World Writing: "When I Lose My Taste"
Post Road: "Pin Oak" and "Riding in the Back"
Raven Chronicles: "The Business of Trains"
James Dickey Review: "My Closest Brush with Anarchy"
Rattle: "Apron Strings," "Levels of Shit," and "Second Marriage I" (under the title "Second Marriage")
Stag Hill Literary Journal: "Trust," "What We Make," and "Second Marriage III" (under the title "Second Marriage")
Stone, River, Sky: An Anthology of Georgia Poems: "Narcissus" and "Winter to Spring"
Tar River Review: "My Father Drowning"

Also thanks to the editors of *Verse Daily* for reprinting "Apron Strings," "Made Bed," and "Soldier Heart"

Jennifer Wheelock and Cathy Carlisi, this manuscript would not exist without you—your inspiration, your brilliant critical feedback and your constant, unwavering support. Tom Forsthoefel, my life's love and my champion, thank you for the beautiful 'second' of us. Beth Castrodale, you bear witness to the powers of friendship and persistence; we are sisters through words. Carey Scott Wilkerson, with thanks for your enthusiastic brilliance and your unwavering belief in the transformational power of art. Beto and Robert Cumming, thank you, thank you for believing in these poems. Jericho Brown, David Lehman and Paisley Rekdal, honored is too small a word. Susan White, Sheri Joseph, Jessica Handler and Peter McDade—thank you for being so all-around fabulous as writers and people—you can't know how much I learn from each of you. Thanks to Julie Bloemeke for her kind words and support. And thanks to Georgia State University, my amazing and talented colleagues and students, who inspire me on a daily basis, particularly Lynee Gaillet for her unwavering support and for finagling time off for me to work on this manuscript and live with my husband. Finally, thanks to my parents, Mary Ann and Carl Kowalski, for your steadfast love and for teaching me how to live fully and well and have fun along the way.

Contents

I

When Touch Does Not Feel • 13

· · ·

My Closest Brush with Anarchy • 15
Made Bed • 16
Second Marriage • 17
Second Marriage (II) • 18
Second Marriage (III) • 20
Anglerfish • 21
House Purchase • 22
Trust • 24

II

When I Lose My Taste • 29

· · ·

Segments • 31
Levels of Shit • 32
The Purpose • 33
Drinking Brother Blues • 35
A Friendship • 36
Lurching My Way to Paradise • 38
Winter to Spring • 39
Market Forces • 40
"Wine the Liquid Cure for Tax Time" • 41

III

When I Am Blind • 45

· · ·

Conundrum • 47
Narcissus • 48
Pin Oak • 49
Riding in the Back • 50
Riding Lessons • 51
Crooked Lines • 54
The Business of Trains • 55

Working Your Way to The Top • 56
Scaffold • 57
Not Exactly • 59
Daily Bread • 60

IV

Mute • 63
• • •
Monastic • 65
The Catholic Schoolgirl Learns to Talk Dirty • 66
Our Father of Perpetual Sadness • 68
Study Abroad • 69
How to Lose • 70
Ways to See • 72
Apron Strings • 73
Ways of Falling • 74
My Father Drowning • 75
Bikini Waxes and Taxes • 76
Sirens • 78

V

Backwash

1. Unmoored • 81
2. Sinking • 82
3. Deeper • 83
4. Adrift • 84
5. Run Aground • 85
6. Rip Tide • 86
7. Undertow • 87

Soldier Heart • 88

for Cathy Carlisi and Jennifer Wheelock

I

*We don't exist unless we are deeply and sensually
in touch with that which can be touched but not known.*

—D. H. Lawrence

When Touch Does Not Feel

How will I know smooth or slick, the edge
of a button, coarse fur, the lip's dry
thin against the tongue tip? How will I know
when, in the dark bed, you reach for me?
Each time, you'll have to say my name
till its blunt syllable prods me awake.

Watch me plunge my hands into boil,
or sink needles in the plush of a palm.
I'll be a trick pony, a circus freak,
slicing my forearms with the sharpened
blade of a machete, or holding lit matches
to my chin until it burnishes and bubbles.

Maybe you can teach me the song of the skin,
my deaf fingers hearing through curve,
my stunted nerves finding voice through
counterpoint of pressure: *"this way—this way,"*
my nipples pinking, my shadows grown moist,
despite that all my wiring's shorted,
despite that if you cut me, I don't cry.

(Touch)

My Closest Brush with Anarchy

Briefly, in grad school,
I had three lovers
at the same time:
one married, one
in another state,
and one who knew
but didn't care.
Terrified but so alive
I couldn't sleep, I felt
constantly short of breath,
my legs thin from the miles
I ran to keep from crazy—
thoughts in my head
tumbling like numbers
in a bingo wheel,
even as cotton
sleeves were peeled
from arms like the skins
of fruit, even as tongues
slid along the edges
of edges, even as I rose
and fell, rose and fell
like a car on a Ferris wheel
that runs all night,
light panning the sky
as I lifted from one lonely
space to the next,
thinking, *love, love, love...*

Made Bed

He could have been my lover again that night—
a whisper of dress lifting over ears,
the tie unknotting, the sheets predictably white,

the fumbling urgency leaving us breathless, light
from lust tinged by guilt, the vanished years.
He could have been my lover again that night,

confusing past with present, desire with flight,
image with image: elbow, breastbone, sheers—
the tie unknotted, the sheets ironically white.

Entangled, our voices pitching like a kite
in a storm with vowels, bleats, stifled swears....
He could have been my lover again that night

if the night were only and alone, if right
and right had not had different names. Affairs:
the ties unknotting, the sheets iconically white

and damp, and something's broken, lost, bright
as shattered glass, as side-lit, backstage mirrors.
He could have been my lover again that night,
the ties unknit, the sheets shamelessly white.

Second Marriage

The day you proposed,
the crows nesting
beside your house
screamed human screams.
You handed me rings
lodged in a box
that looked like a miniature house.
We ran six miles, both of us
thinner from worry and surprise.
I wept and joked about divorce—
my tongue turned wood, my brain
a Tilt-A-Whirl, Cuisinart.
We toasted with bourbon.
What to eat to celebrate
a second engagement? Bologna?

Hold my hand and close your eyes.
How to even think of a veil,
a clutch of tulips or begonias?
Grandmother's wedding dress
has tiny holes chewed
by mice or moths. In July,
you'll wear your only sports coat,
all wool. The courthouse steps
strewn with trash, we'll snag
a witness down the street
pissing in the holly.

Second Marriage II

His youngest cried, his daughter slammed the phone,
his son called him self-absorbed, his ex
left sixteen voicemails on his cell—fifty
minutes of complaints and threats—

               and we were sleepless,
alternately weeping, pooled in sweat,
the heat wave caught us air-condition free,
a little lost, although we knew we'd waited
long enough, and when he asked, with open
box, I'd felt a fist break loose, a flower
blooming white and damp and vivid, as if
I'd learned how orchids grow.

•

We'd marry the weekend Erie held its yearly
Roar Along the Shore: twenty thousand
bikers from out of town—tattoo Virgin
Marys, a pink Harley Cadillac,
a rider with a pug in his sidecar.

•

We never hired a gypsy to check for hair
inside a newly broken egg. Still,
I glanced to heaven for hurtling broomsticks
when the judge asked if anyone objected.
The sky was clear—blue as a baby's eyes.

We did. We would. In minutes we were off
to Raj Majal to raise our dollar flutes
and down our saag paneer, the gin martinis
that his friends brought and made too strong,

so Mom, who hadn't eaten lunch, got sick,
and all of us were tipsy or giddy, filled
with thanks, curry, a sheet cake bought at Kroger.

•

After, we lay in his apartment napping,
numb with exhaustion and relief.

•

At four, two mornings later, a hot crack split
a tree just feet from where we lay. Alarm
about to sound, the lights flashed then went. We packed
in darkness, hoping we had what we'd need.

Second Marriage III

my mouth is too full   except
that he has lifted only a shovel
a suitcase in the ten years
I've known him   he would
carry me over   I can never
be carried   don't you see
I have bureaus   balanced
on my back   summer
and the moon   sweeping
across the gray stretch
as if to wave   I have always
only   been leaving
until he found me   here
which is anywhere   which is
what I mean when I wake
and his hands   I would change
for him   they say that doesn't
happen   or is it shouldn't
anyway   he too harbored a moon
and he could cook   who wouldn't
tie that knot   before   I kept
looking back   as if I had dropped
a glove on the sidewalk   before him
cloth for my fingers   now this

Anglerfish

You'd never guess it was her second marriage,
every sentence marked now with a "we,"
as in: "Thank God, *at last* we booked a florist,"
and, "We've tried to keep it small, but couldn't *not*
invite his father's partners; then several cousins
are flying in from France—we're thrilled, of course…
We both want kids. We're fighting over names
already." She pauses. Her eyes focus on something
in the air, "We hope our first's a girl…"

I think of the anglerfish, whose angry grimace
grazes the deep sea floor, the young male,
smaller in size, finds himself a female
and latches on. His sharp teeth embedded,
eventually his lips become absorbed,
their vessels fuse, his eyes and organs lost.
She wears him like an arm or strange appendage.
He becomes so wholly her the only
part of him that finally lasts are testes,
the only part of him she really needs.

House Purchase

Instead of "Adding Wife to Deed"
I read "Adding Wife to Dead,"

and think of my body hoisted
by the tongs of a pitchfork

onto a pile of previous somebodies,
then the open bed of a truck

bouncing the thick density of dead
against its sides or each other,

noses flattened, fingers splayed
as it rolls down some pocked

and pitted road, its ditches
lined with empty wine bottles,

discarded socks, a leather laceless
shoe—the metal circles of its eyes.

Further on, the field is mostly mud,
and we are jacked at an angle

before sliding down the steel flatness,
our faces abrading, thunking in muck

like deflated footballs—buttocks
breasts, elbows, a welter of limbs

all splayed like used dolls, and the tires
backing away as the driver balances

his arm against the window frame,
calls the wife to ask what's for dinner,

guns out of the sludge where the bodies
remain—blunt, dumb lumps—

as he heads toward their bungalow,
where his two teen boys wait on the porch

playing their favorite game: *how long
can I choke you before you scream?*

Trust

He cradles my head midair,
his fingers, slow pistons

stroking my throat, and then
they are on the trachea,

the pressure definite, my breath
impeded ever so slightly.

This is the week a pilot
slammed the nose of a plane

into the side of a mountain.
This is the week the Boston

Marathon bomber watched impassively
while jury members examined

the items used to make the bombs:
pressure cooker, ignition powder,

the inside mechanism
of a Christmas tree light bulb.

I've run several marathons,
stepped hundreds of times

onto a plane, rarely doubting
I would reach my destination,

and I think how easy
this man I've paid to help

tame my stress could clamp down—
he is so strong—crush off

the flow that moves as seamlessly
as the music, some sitar-plucking,

Indian-sounding track that plays
in a loop as the incense burns,

and the man with his calm voice,
almost whispers to me

my name, as his fingers again
stutter the wind of my body.

II

*One must ask children and birds
how cherries and strawberries taste.*

—Johann Wolfgang von Goethe

When I Lose My Taste

I will press my tongue to brick—
in my cottage, paint every wall
and floor a shade of yellow.

Ravenous as a bear in spring,
I will chew clover and marzipan
and every breed of nut, bake cakes
with foreign names: Strueselkuchen,
Bebinca, Buccellato, Sachertorte.

Each nerve a point of desire.
I will ache till my vision blurs,
my throat's all screech and rasp.

I will raise my hands to the light.
And the light will drop like a quarter
in a pond, and the music, sweet as cane,
will filter through the pines.

May God lift me under my arms
and carry me where he must.
May wings remind me
of chocolate and cardamom.

May mornings recall butter
and raspberry, cabernet and framboise,
the taste of your lips, fog beyond the lighthouse,
that sweep of arm guiding us all along.

(Taste)

Segments

the morning before   his hands
split   the closed   scissors of my thighs,
my friend   Jeannie and i ate
cake   grapefruit sized oranges
picked   from giant trays of them
tempting   at the outdoor market.

we walked the beach chattering
about what   twenty something
women   chatter   about on break
in Greece   mostly   the two hot
Canadians we'd met   would later see
that night   the sun's   steady hand
heavy at our backs   we strolled
then ran   shrieking   laughing
when an old man   without a suit
snarl of   white pubic hair   walked
unabashedly   straight   out of the waves.

silenced   the next morning   i
dazed   by the too bright
light   and what he hadn't   understood
of no   not   laughed it off
when Jeannie asked   *what*   *happened*
with your date   *why*   *are you*   *so*
quiet   *strange*   the orange   again
so huge   sweet even still   i taste
it   bursting in my mouth

Levels of Shit

for the politicians

Winters, the round brown
balls of manure would
fall steaming in untidy piles,
the horses unperturbed,
their noses in a bucket of sweet feed,
or grazing the dusty floors
of their stalls, simply lifted
their tails and let loose.
Later, those same stones,
frozen, thrown well and hard,
might have shattered
someone's window. It was easy
to trip on one, random rolled
into the barn aisle: innocent,
icy rocks of shat grain we shoveled
or pitchforked into wheelbarrows,
dumped in a pile, their fragrance
diminished in the subzero temperatures,
though the mountains we'd raise
before the tractor hauled them away
were impressive. The horses
continued to eat and excrete,
and we kept scooping. We didn't worry
what came out of assholes.
We recycled that shit. Something
now I can't imagine as I sit
watching this screen, and it comes
from another hole, with no way
to pile or pass along or diminish.

The Purpose

After hearing Arun Ghandi speak on world hunger
Global Purpose Summit (3/4/2014)

By the time you read this line,
small children have starved
to their death, men have been shot.
If I keep going, the scars of the planet
will overwhelm you; you may need
to play a game of Angry Birds,
finish your Sudoku, put away
the clean dishes. Children are dying.
They keep dying. What can you do,
but wash a load of laundry?
What can you do, but kiss
the forehead of your baby girl
when she shows you the picture
of the sun and the orange-haired boy
and the small blue pond, like a long
blue squash flattened on the ground
that is part of the world where
children are dying and keep
dying? You can't stop thinking
of how many babies you can't save.
No matter how much money you send
in an envelope, the minute
you mail it, there's another
dozen gone, then another. Don't
push it from your head, let it
sit there, the idea: another, another.
You are probably getting hungry, and still
another, another, and you need
to eat a sandwich, even though by now
you feel bad about the sandwich,
the hunger. It's not going to bring you
down to your knees the way it has and does
those children—another, another,
into infinity, and still you have to eat
your ham sandwich with provolone,

and lettuce, and mustard, and no onion,
and you have to flush, and you have to live
the way you have lived your whole
life, while another—then another—
gone and gone and gone.

Drinking Brother Blues

He was in a spot of trouble, my brother,
waking drunk, declaring himself fine,
stumbling to the sink for some water,

his head a puzzle he couldn't piece together,
his wife hysterical, *You've crossed the line!*
He was in a peck of trouble, my brother,

wife on the phone declaiming to her mother,
I told him, he's got to go. He felt insane
staring at the sink, the running water,

with no way to unfold the metal bumper,
uncrush the neighbor's mailbox, undrink the wine.
He was in a wad of trouble, my brother.

Thank god the kids were out of town for summer
camp. He'd make this right, he thought, again,
leaning against the sink, splashing water

in his face, determined. He'd promise better,
sober, no more secrets, no more pain.
He was in a heap of trouble, my brother,
at the sink, wanting more than water.

A Friendship

Slicing the stem of a plant
that bled a white froth
the color of milk,
burying a dead mouse
in an old shoe box—how we
read from the Bible,
making the sign of the cross;
pedaling hard without helmets
down steep Sylvania Drive,
mouths open, unbrushed
knotted hair flying back.
So much screaming.
Licking snot drips from upper lips,
filthy hands digging
cookies from the jar.
Playing dress-up: Mom's
necklace snapping
from our hands, the pearls
rolling beneath her bed
and heavy dresser. Huge
pink welts from mosquitoes.
That beach trip—sunburn so bad
we rubbed ice against our cheeks.
Smashing together Barbie and Ken's
ungenitaled nakedness.
Trying to flush Ken
down the toilet. Sleepovers:
talking so long and hard
we'd fall asleep still mumbling.
After your move, not wanting
to even drive past your house.
My bus trip to see you beside a man
so fat my smashed arm
lost its feeling. Writing letters

about school and boys,
annoying new friends.
Summer and Christmas visits,
faces pressed against glass,
weeks lost like a wave of a hand,
that first metallic taste of lonely.

Lurching My Way to Paradise

*The path to paradise
begins in hell.*
—Dante

on a Greyhound bus,
Pittsburgh to Erie, cold drizzle

slicking our steel-clad sides,
gag-thick raft of B.O. cresting

from the seat behind me.
A young woman two seats up

wears mismatched pajamas,
stares toward a window—

runway thin, head a bouquet
of dreads, offset mouth

like a figure painted by Picasso.
A man across the aisle swallows

something from a bag.
A woman with ear buds

smiles faintly, nods and nods.
As exhaust fumes simmer

with the sour of sweat,
a random plastic bottle rolling,

then stopping, then spinning
again beneath the clotted

rows of seats, what song
inspiring *yes* can't I hear?

Winter to Spring

Each year the dull colors
seep into you like the sound
of a sigh. You awaken
heavy; you go to sleep heavy.
The drenched, glaucous
heft of the sky squats
on your happy like a stuck pig.
Sickly, plucked, you manage,
with great effort, to stand,
to eat, to move through days
as if through coagulate slop.

Finally, the sun's
pistons start
to fire again—
you feel yourself
unspooling—
something inside you
is breaking apart.

Then, one day, like a switch
flicked to light up the stage—
presto!—outside a flurry of bird
and blossom, buzz and whiff, each smell,
flavor tugging your nose a different
direction, and color everywhere:
lavender, periwinkle, chiffon, chartreuse…
every angle a suffusion, spores of pollen
thickening the air until the whole world
is slightly out of focus, and you are
dizzy, breathless with *alive*.

Market Forces

> *The Mount Washington Kroger is out of Bananas*
> —newspaper headline

Yes, we have no bananas today,
but Cheetos and nacho chips—
seven different brands—and instant
mashed potatoes complete with sodium
acid pyrophosphate, and sodium bisulfite.
We have Gummi bears and red cinnamon
candy hearts. Ranch dressing, a whole row
of plastic-wrapped, sliced meat. Line up
for your diacetyl, your free glutamic acid,
your butylated hydroxyanisole.
We have everything but bananas,
those bright phallic bunches; those wrapped
wands of fruit-meat; potassium
hunger bombs; soft, sweet monkey crack.

"Wine the Liquid Cure for Tax Time"

advertisement for wine.com

Hello, uncorked spirit, my ruby elixir,
my evening's closer, savory light, rest.
Hello, my tax-burdened, work-dulled fixer.
Take me to your gardens, with its breasts
of swelled fruit shirking behind leaves,
where I'll curl in the shadows like a pod,
absorb dirt's cool knowing—no fraud
in chlorophyll or the unsensed heaves
of earth's rotation. Oh life juice, oh sauce
that stirs loins, let me climb back
along the curved map of your vines
to taste grit and the sun's gloss—
salt and iron rising in the veins—
to plunge as deep as possible into black.

III

Close both eyes to see with the other eye.

—Rumi

When I am Blind

When I am blind, colors will smell
of lemon and apricot and sage.
With my fingertips, I will read your body
the way a cook reads the skin
of ready fruit. Delicious
will be my paradigm. I will ache
for trees, the sieve of a young moon
severing the dark. The moon will live
inside me then. Planting its feet
in the pit of me, it will shine
through my mouth, warm-tongued,
electric. I will wish for nothing,
consumed by memory: rock,
churned butter, fur, vermilion.
I will clothe myself in shades
I'd never recognize. Only birds
will know the sky the way I do.

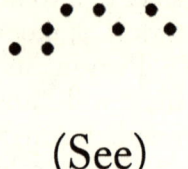

(See)

Conundrum

Why are scars sexy?
Is it the suggestion
of the body opened up—

the body built of cavities?
Is it the hint
of something missing—

the jagged reminder
of an ever-looming end?
Once, my gut was a smooth

downy globe. Now
marked with a thick
brown line left by a scalpel,

it beckons wandering
fingers or tongues,
like the lips of a seam,

to unzip or tug apart.
I am whole but broken,
maimed but healed.

The pound-heavy melon
of cells removed,
I am less and more.

Narcissus

In clusters, the slender,
girlish stems thrust
almond-shaped tips
up through the dirt,
while tentacle legs
lower unseen into banks,
along ridges, in rows
at the edges of yards.

Soon, sun-glazed
or etched by the cool
droplets that they later
drink through their feet
like a party trick,
their minds explode
into electric gold
show-stoppers, coronas,
fanned by the six,
silk-soft perianth.

Mornings, their pale,
diaphanous faces
lean toward the burn,
and you cup them
with your fingers,
thinking, *Who wouldn't
bend before the water
to worship this?*

Pin Oak

It bends rooted in its fury
of silence, its trunk with not
one straight section,
its bark, gnarled and pocked.
You can't keep your eye
from the grotesque growths
that mar its surfaces:
raised elliptical scars
that look like the lips
of screaming mouths,
where limbs have been hacked off
or chewed loose by the wind's
invisible teeth. How
is it still standing with pale,
green sickly leaves
sprouting from branches
that miraculously drape
to the ground but still hold on?

It is like the man's body
so wracked and wrecked
by the years, his back cannot
unbend itself. The man
smiles as he tries to unfurl
above the insect-like
apparatus of a walker,
a figure who used to stand
six foot two, who could down
a tall pine with several
swift strikes from an ax,
who is your mother's father,
your grandfather, a man,
who, decades earlier,
entered a room and turned
every woman's eyes.

Riding in the Back

The cat cries at the snapped tab of a can.
The baby reaches for the dangling key.
The man pours a drink when he hears
his mother's name. And you
think of horses when you ride in the back
of your father's Avalon, of galloping
over shrubs and grassy fields toward
each line of fence you drive past,
leaning forward, the leather reins
taut in your hands, the horse's outstretched
legs spewing chunks of turf.

You are carried within sound: hoof
and heart and wind, and as you reach
the line, you rise slightly, the horse slows,
gathers on its haunches, springs forward.
You cling to the beast and are flung
like a toy over each barrier, long
lengths of wood or wire. In your head
you gallop toward the next property
divider, then the next, even though
you have not stepped in a stirrup in years.

Riding Lessons

Back in sixth grade, before
cell phones, before texting,

before computers and the internet,
Tina Romano became my best friend.

Slender, pale, eyes like those
of a dog at the pound—wet, dark, scared—

she lived on the side of town where
trailers were randomly planted at angles,

where my first love—horses—
munched clover in un-mown pastures,

and we could ride for hours
on trails cut through the nearby woods.

Eight people lived in her small,
three bedroom, aluminum-sided ranch,

decorated inside with saints and doilies,
a space often ringing with *shit* and *hell*,

bitch and *dammit*....words I would never
repeat at home. If they knew, I imagined

my parents' heads popping like balloons.
I loved the shouting—so different

from my own placid, suburban family—
the smell of red sauce always simmering

on their rusting, brown, electric stove,
her mother, with big hair,

big hips, cursing like Mick Jagger. Evenings,
one of us would call the other, and we'd talk

an hour, sometimes two, though we spent
most afternoons together at the barn.

One day, she arrived at school
shoulders heaving, eyes red

and wider than usual, her epileptic sister
rushed to the hospital the previous night,

so sick she might not make it,
the niece and nephew, soon to be

without a mom, the gross brother-in-law,
their only parent, the one who'd asked

to touch Tina's breasts. I hugged her.
What did I know of trouble?

No wonder the next year
when Jackie moved to her street—

Jackie of the long red hair—
Jackie from downtown,

who took *nothing from no one*,
whose brothers aimed their sling shots

at our hips, whose father was building
their whole house *with his bare hands*,

would become the preferred.
We all rode together—

Jackie now too—her horse
an ornery appaloosa who kicked

or bit if we got too close.
Tina almost never called anymore,

and I usually sat on the bus
in the seat in front of them,

as they joked, hunched shoulder-
to-shoulder, and tried

to keep up, asking, *What's so funny?*,
or laughing, pretending

to get it, as we bounced
our way to the barn.

Crooked Lines

The woman boarding the train, seized
by the grip of an ongoing tremor, steps forward

tentatively, stumblingly, suitcase dragging
behind her, then catching on a corner, then

lurching free as she shuffles, twists, awkwardly
lands in the seat just across from me, doughy,

sixtyish, curly hair haloing her face, she has
a sweetness that defies expectation, her bobble

head perpetually nodding and smiling gently,
as if to accept, sorrowfully, the train and all

its occupants, as if to forgive the child crying
a few rows in front of us, the tatted-up man,

slick-shiny, black pants so tight he must
roll them on like a condom, the women shrieking

with laughter, one so amused by what
her friend is saying, she stands and pounds

her knee with her hand, and even me—
the nodding, half-smiling, seraphic face

seeming to comb out some snag, some
trouble, some deep, embedded tangle.

The Business of Trains

The rain might turn to ice later tonight,
but today a tree by the train track
has buds the exact size and shape
of the ends of human fingers. So many
ways to be tortured, but I once fainted
watching a dog have its tooth pulled.
Tonight the ice might fall, but today
the sun nudges its bald face through a cloud,
and I run past that tree with all of my fingers,
my toes. At home, I will gather candles
and whiskey. I will try to remember
gratitude—if a branch crashes
through the roof, if the lights flicker
to darkness, if we are snowbound
and chattering—I will toast the many
digits that are mine, and the train
whistling down a track that does not carry
those who will soon become smoke,
as so many have and do and will.

Working Your Way to the Top

NO.
think,
the pile and
stand before
Sometimes, you
like a broken toy.
just churn your arms
each aside. Sometimes, you
useless item to the next, pushing
you methodically move from one
the hard rim of a blender. Sometimes,
televisions, computer screens, armchairs,
grasping for something solid: antennas of old
Each day is a landfill you must claw your way through,

Scaffold

Prehistoric, all bone, they loom

above us along city blocks,

as tiny insects of men

crawl along their spines,

or balance there, wielding

paintbrushes or squeegees,

or sitting beside a palate

of red brick, legs dangling

like a child's legs from a swing.

The men are usually so high

we can't hear their whistles

or sneezes. Even eating lunch,

they wear hats, the reflections

of their faces blotted by clouds

or haloed by sun, or on cold

winter mornings, their features

fading to grim. Some days, I wish

to live with them in the sky,

swimming in light, breathing

buildings and silt, nearly birds

they are so delicate laboring in air.

Not Exactly

We asked for soft as flannel,
touching ourselves with fingertips
to show what we meant,

but the outcomes were scratchy
or textured. We said, "No, no, no.
like this," attempting to explain,

to exhibit, to diagram—our only choice
to keep trying. We made faces;
we wrote in block letters across the walls;

someone even stood on a desk
to make the point, stamping his feet,
violently waving his arms. Outside,

the skies had turned a vibrant
shade of ochre—the clouds
split by the sun's burning baldness

as it sank—so lovely we stopped
for a minute to watch. Still,
it wasn't quite what we wanted.

Daily Bread

Not eyesome, the houses
      with their crooked shutters
            and paint peeling, roof tiles
curling at the edges;

nor the yards, patches
      of red dirt, onion grass
            popping up
like tufts of hair after chemo;

nor the residents
      milling about by the park,
            or walking their pit bulls,
their chows.

Plastic bags from fast food by the curb,
      random chicken bones, random
            condoms, wire hangers, discarded
remnants of damaged furniture.

Still, the man perches
      every day on his lawn chair
            at the corner of his lot,
dressed often in a suit,

cane balanced at his knee,
      his thick, grey mustache,
            walnut skin, accordioned at the eyes,
smiles broadly when I jog past,

raises a wavering hand.

IV

*It requires wisdom to understand wisdom:
the music is nothing if the audience is deaf.*

—Walter Lippmann

Mute

Each of my gestures a homily,
I will tattoo you with my eyes,
tongue you with my black
hole of need. My speech the gut's
twisted ache—the pause
as the conductor raises his arms,
the space between ticks of a clock.

Like a departed train, its engine
steam a cool disappearance,
timber and mulch hoarding
its clatter and moan, I have left you
at the station. I am the unmarked staff
that waits for dark notes, all yours.

⠐⠓⠑⠜

(Hear)

Monastic

Silence—the gristle
on which I chewed
day after day.

I can't describe the taste.
Have you studied the space
between leaves on a tree?

Daily, we worked in the garden
side by side. I treasured each
labored breath of my brothers,
each small grunt.

I befriended a spider in the corner
of my window—carcasses
of flies drying on the sill.

Did I meet God? I understood less
more clearly. God's
patience—my common prayer.

The Catholic Schoolgirl Learns to Talk Dirty

"Fuck me," she whispers
to the mirror, holds her face

as close as she can
to watch the way her lips

move, the 'f' of her teeth
hitting the top of her lower lip,

the 'k' at the back of her throat,
sounds as strange to her

as the man she once saw
with an extra mouth

on the side of his head.
She needs an extra mouth

to say the words she can't,
cock and *suck* and *do me*

like you want it, baby.
Puffy mouth with full

painted lips like a porn star's,
should speak in a way that sends

nuns into confessionals
or drives her husband to distraction

as he teaches the intricacies
of Eastern ascetic poets:

how, according to Rumi,
"Only from the heart

can you touch the sky,"
how you must "…close

both eyes to see
with the other eye."

Our Father of Perpetual Sadness

Father Frederick's smile has gone away.
Too much adultery, divorce and death.
Too many congregants for whom to pray.

First, the deacon's son went missing (they say
his T-cell count is low), then Sister Ruth
got caught with Fr. Chet. (They've run away.)

God seems more distant in church each Sunday
with charges filed and brother Conrad's health
in jeopardy, our flock kneels to pray:

for shut-ins, the poor, those who've wandered astray—
we lower heads, our voices all one breath.
But Father Frederick's smile has gone away.

It hurts to look at him. We've lost our way.
Still, he preaches we must maintain our faith—
reminds us weekly about the need to pray.

"The Lord redeems and loves," he'll always say,
yet when I see his face, I feel the earth
is like to buck. His smile has gone away,
and I don't know who listens when we pray.

Study Abroad

One of my flat-mates, a thin,
pretty woman, older, proper,
studying to be a nurse, had lost

her father not two years before.
The kitchen conversation turned
to the subject of death, not the father,

exactly, though I should have known
he was sitting there at the table:
his watery eyes, his kindness, the way

he must have touched her cheek.
Lorna was her name. Lorna.
A name I'd never heard in America.

She was Scottish. He must have
loved to say it to himself and to her,
the lilt in his voice making a slight gulp

on the 'R.' They adored each other.
I know because I started to say—adamant
as any know-it-all, twenty-year-old

from America—that the survivors
of the dead have a selfish hurt, a hurt
about themselves, because the dead,

are dead. They don't have feelings.
She paled, then pinked, arguing, "No,
it isn't that way. We mourn for all

the person didn't get to have or see
or do, for the life they couldn't live."
She slammed her hand on the table.

She was weeping, and her father
placed his over top of its trembling,
as I stopped talking for once in my life.

How to Lose

You can lose a friend
when you don't

kiss her back, when she leans
forward, and you turn

your chin like you've
smelled a bad smell.

When she comes over
for a drink, angles

sideways, her bangs
falling across her face,

confess to her about
your married lover,

a man she's known
for years. Tell her

what you did
between library stacks;

describe your fingers
curling against spines.

Notice she is wearing
a knit sweater that shows off,

with its light, plum pill,
the swell of her breasts.

Lose her calm stare as she listens
and doesn't blink,

how she places a cool hand
on your forehead

as you weep. Lose it all.

Ways to See

"Amy Jones." The professor said it twice.
It's Ma-yatt, a voice wavered from beneath the brim
of a blue baseball hat, the sound thin,
a drawl as southern as sweet potato pie.
He sat at the back, slumping in his chair the way
the athletes did. Pretty and petite, he'd mastered
a bad boy smirk, deflection with humor, the swagger
of someone defended but tough—I'd like to say
I didn't stare. The professor made a note
and carried on with class; she read us a poem
about a man who shot his dogs then shot
himself after learning he'd lost his farm. No one
responded, then from the back, that twang: "Them dawgs.
He loved 'em." "That's right, Matt. He loved those dogs."

Apron Strings

I have lied about my mother.
She never wore aprons,
regularly burned dinners.
A student and teacher
with four young kids, she broke
multiple watches—wound
too tight—made lists she'd forget
on countertops and tables.

Forever distracted, forever
rushing about with heels
in one hand, a baby in the other,
who could blame her
for not meeting us at the door
with a hug and a cookie?

Number-cruncher, maker
of money, a modern woman
before the phrase was de rigueur,
my mother opened doors
in business and in solitude.
She would shape our lives
forever by leaving us alone.

Ways of Falling

The cinched belt of the hour-glass—
    that week: Amy moved
        into a basement apartment,

done with her stepson's addiction,
    her husband's blind eye,
        Sandy's brother's body

found room temperature,
    bloating, sprawled by the tub
        when the police kicked through the door.

Jen's fragile mom made an appointment
    at the salon to wash the blood from her hair
        after her collapse in the kitchen.

My father couldn't remember the word
    for glass, the word for piano.

We jogged through the neighborhood
    where redbuds puckered purple
        and young mothers

pushing strollers stopped to gossip
    along the sidewalk. We shrugged
        off our sweaters.

We drank margaritas on the porch as the skies
    paled. Two swifts feathered past your head.
        We toasted no answers for anyone.

My Father Drowning

He struggles for a word
the way some men struggle
to catch a fish, the boat
too small, the dark sea's
tongue lapping and lapping
like a dog's at the edge
of the fragile vessel, and when
it finally comes to him,
he can hardly get his lips
around the sound, slippery
sound, his voice so soft we
lean forward. My father,
who, when I was young,
swung me by my arms
safe above the waves,
now neck deep, and I want
to drag him back toward air,
but no one can swim out there,
his sea is only his and so wide
we can sometimes hardly
see him, arms limp by his
sides, lips moving because
he still thinks he can be saved.

Bikini Waxes and Taxes

You don't want to head to Florida
with a Chewbacca crotch,
nor for Congress to pass
a tax cut for the rich.

Terrifying thoughts: tufts
weaseling out the edges
of your bathing suit, billionaires
with blond wives posing
behind placards of dollar bills.

There is need, and there is
need. You go see Rosa
from Brazil, whose art
involves nudity and pain,

who is unfazed by your
spread-legged shame,
who stares at your privates
like they're a mission.

You suck in your breath
as she slathers the searing wax
on your nether regions,
the same day the Senate scrawls
numbers in the margins—
more zeroes than you can comprehend.

There is debt, and there is debt,
and you will not scream
as she coaches: *breathe, breathe*—
your hair yanked by the root,
follicles bleeding.

The rich, whose wardrobes cost more
than most families' net worth,
say *trickle* and *down*—throw crumbs
to the plebes from the decks of their yachts.

The bald, stinging pink will heal.
The poor will continue to be poorer.

Sirens

They are the swan song of the city,
buildings racked by the long high notes

endure bravely the harrowing soprano
that shakes their many rectangular eyes.

Oh, the city is filled with these strange
cacophonous wails that at times

seem everywhere—ferocious
crescendos echoing and advancing—

and at times seem a note of singular
pathos: throaty, lingering, the noise

thick and juicy as a good cut of beef.
And now you hear them joining

as they must, the United Chorus
of Canines, their untrained voices

rising in sympathy from backyards
and from alleys, dog parks and driveways,

intensely lifting their chins to confirm:
poor you, poor you, poor you, poor you…

V

Ever has it been that love knows not its own depth until the hour of separation.

—Kahlil Gibran

• • •

The heart was made to be broken.

—Oscar Wilde

Backwash

1. Unmoored

He found the gift after she died, still wrapped,
a framed black and white from her trip to Prague,
buried in the closet of their bedroom.
He knew it was a sign from her and wept
lifting it from tissue paper and its tomb
of bubble wrap. He held it to the light:
a moored boat in silhouette, the rod
of its mast halving a mottled sky, a slight
echo of sun through layers of shadowy gray.

The loss was like a stone that cracks a windshield,
and every casserole they brought, each cake,
each heart-felt note, spread webbed cracks across the field
of who he was. He had no anchor now.
He balanced the little print beside the window.

2. Sinking

He balanced the little print beside the window
near where their final Christmas tree had been.
Six weeks he couldn't take it down. He'd go
to get the boxes, then stop. At some point, the thin
branches would break. Still, the days ticked by,
and all ten feet of shine and bobble—lone sign
of before, content, right, and reasons why—
remained. The whole basement smelled of pine
and looked bipolar: part holiday, part packing
to leave, papers and boxes and photos spined
the walls. The day he finally caved—wrapping
each bell and bauble collected for years—he'd find
the stand roped to what was left of it,
stripped and drooping, brown, gone to shit.

3. Deeper

Stripped and drooping, brown, gone to shit—
He sees himself in every branch and needle.
The neighbors are coming. He has to stop, sit,
breathe, change his shirt, make a feeble
attempt to seem fine. He feels like… what?
He feels like nothing he can name. The space
she's left, impossible, each room fraught:
four half-stale, toll-house cookies, that floral vase,
her blouse still draped across the rocker. The knot
of no and nevermore defeats him,
a constant, fervent twisting in his gut.
The neighbors bring soup, knocking on the door.
They take the tree; they take the tree; they take…
that last happy, but the center does not break.

4. Drift

That last happy, but the center does not break.
He picks up groceries, writes a check, calls
his oldest friend. The tasks, tiresome, they make
the time go quickly until they don't. The walls
come down and he's adrift again, alone,
lost in a fog of grief—the food
tasteless, the house a shell, all echo and bone.
The sky becomes a canvas of his mood—
its winter palette mostly gray on gray—
it droops, sodden, cloth-like, hinting of mush.
Even the snow, first white, devolves to slush,
a filthy, blackish soup that car tires spray.
He feeds the birds, the surviving koi, it's late,
bitter, heavy on him, the color, slate.

5. Run Aground

Bitter, heavy on him, the color, slate.
He wakes determined to cook a healthy meal—
his daughter and doctor all on him, he's losing weight.
It's hard to care—he eats to eat now. Still
she wants him to. He feels her in the room
and on the stairway, slight pressure like a thumb
against his arm. A rustle across the carpet.
He wears her favorite scarf —so soft—wombs
himself at night in blankets, folds her unwashed
shirt beneath his head and tries to forget.
She's everywhere and nowhere, he says. *Like God.*
It catches in his throat. He feels bug-like, squashed
by what he doesn't know of her: her thoughts,
her past. Their stuff around him vibrates, rots.

6. Rip Tide

Their past, their stuff around him vibrates, rots.
Focus. Butter the toast. Pour the coffee. Jot
a list of all you have to do: CALL
PASTOR, ORDER FLOWERS, LOOK FOR WILL.
He circles the words he's printed all in caps,
turns to a box he hasn't opened. Its flaps
tucked shut, inside a morass of bills and letters.
He reaches in to extract a random letter,
written to a man he doesn't know. It's old,
brittle, but her perfect cursive loops are clear,
its signature closing: "I couldn't love you more."
I couldn't love you more.... A shock of cold
and then the shout tears through him loud and long—
both him and not him—the roar of all things wrong.

7. Undertow

Both him and not him, the roar of all things wrong,
the sound is like a wave he rides to shore,
knees scraped raw on sand, shaky at the core.
He stands, then sits, then stands. Friends say he's strong.
He isn't. *Just stubborn,* he thinks. The days pass
and he's still here. She's not. *She's not. She's not.*
She used to visit her mom, and he's had the thought
she's just away and coming back, the loss
not real, but then he reaches for her at night
and startles awake to feel a draft of cold,
the mattress a vacant raft without her weight,
her heat, her chest rising beneath the rumpled
sheet. No magic to bring her to their bed—
an unwrapped breathing gift. She is still dead.

Soldier Heart

When you lose your heart, its impossible
drum continues filling ventricles,

a hundred thousand times a day,
two thousand gallons of blue type A

siphon in and out of its four-
chambered machine, threading through more

than sixty thousand miles of veins,
from lung to tissue, tongue to brain.

you stand—despite that you can't stand—
despite that your unwilling hand

touches the casket's closed lid—this fist
bumps, bumps like victory in your chest.

—Lia Paprocki

A Professor at Georgia State University and award-winning writer, Beth Gylys has published three collections of poetry (*Sky Blue Enough to Drink, Spot in the Dark* and *Bodies that Hum*) and two chapbooks (*Matchbook* and *Balloon Heart*). Recipient of a fellowship to attend the MacDowell Colony, her work has been featured on the *Writers Almanac, Poetry Daily* and *Verse Daily,* and she has had poetry published in many anthologies and journals including *Rattle, Barrow Street, Paris Review, Antioch Review, Kenyon Review, Ploughshares, Boston Review,* and *The Southern Review.*

www.ingramcontent.com/pod-product-compliance
Lightning Source LLC
Chambersburg PA
CBHW022119090426
42743CB00008B/913